"It Must Be Nice to Be Little"

for Emily
with ♡

'83

"It Must Be Nice to Be Little"

A *For Better or For Worse*® Collection

by Lynn Johnston

Andrews and McMeel, Inc.
A Universal Press Syndicate Company
Kansas City • New York

ISBN: 0-8362-1113-8
Library of Congress Catalog Card Number: 83-71767

I t delights me to have the opportunity to live with and know some of the happiest people in the world — cartoonists. They love what they're doing, and it makes their work fun.

Lynn Johnston, for example, is just what you'd hope she'd be. She looks like her cartoon counterpart — she has a family that looks like the family in the strip; her husband, Rod, really is a dentist; and each one of them is just as nice, fun-loving, and warm as you'd expect.

Lynn appears to be writing about your family and mine. But, how can she know what we're all doing since she lives in northern Canada about 150 miles from the Arctic Circle? It's possibly because Lynn laughs and cries along with fan mail from people she has never met, and because the Johnstons have most of the same problems and rewards as the rest of us. Lynn has the remarkable ability, which cartoonists seem to have, that allows her to see each day as a series of humorous and loving moments. And then, somehow, she is able to transform those thoughts magically onto paper.

Maybe if we keep laughing along with Lynn's cartoons, we'll be enriched with her insight on life. And, perhaps, just as we're on the verge of strangling our children, one of Lynn's cartoon balloons will appear above our heads showing us the humor of the situation in time to save us from a regrettable act.

I'm sure you'll enjoy this book, so read on.

—*Carolyn Davis*, mother of a darling three-year-old, wife of Jim (GARFIELD) Davis, and (as of today) writer

I WISH I COULD COME FOR COFFEE, ANNE — BUT THE KIDS ARE STILL SICK.

NO, THEY DON'T HAVE TEMPERATURES... BUT I KNOW THEY'RE NOT VERY WELL.

— THEY HAVEN'T FOUGHT ALL MORNING.

WHEN'S YOUR BROTHER COMING? NEXT WEEK

DOES CONNIE KNOW HER OLD FLAME WILL BE BACK IN TOWN?

YEAH — SHE HEARD THROUGH THE GRAPEVINE.

AND I'M SPEAKING TO THE CHIEF GRAPE!

I THINK YOU'RE WELL ENOUGH TO GO TO SCHOOL TODAY, MICHAEL.

NO, MA! HACK SNORT, KOFF WHEEZE!

AND OOOOH THE PAIN, MA.... THE PAIN!!

I GUESS I OVERACTED.

ANNE! LOOK AT ALL THESE LOVELY LITTLE BABY CLOTHES.

I MUST ADMIT — I AM A BIT JEALOUS.

IT WOULD BE NICE TO BE IN YOUR SHOES.

HERE...THEY HAVEN'T FIT FOR A WEEK!

YES, IT'S FUN BEING PREGNANT AGAIN! — BUYING LITTLE CLOTHES, THINKING OF NAMES....

AND TO THINK I SAID I ONLY WANTED ONE — CRASH!!

ELLY! — WHAT AM I DOING??

YEAH? — FAR OUT! WHAT TIME?

HEY, SIS! — CONNIE'S INVITED ME FOR SUPPER — AND WE MIGHT TAKE IN A SHOW!

I KNOW I DON'T HAVE TO TELL HER EVERYTHING. JUST THOUGHT I'D CLUE HER IN.

IT KEEPS HER FROM LEAVING EAR PRINTS ON THE WALLPAPER.

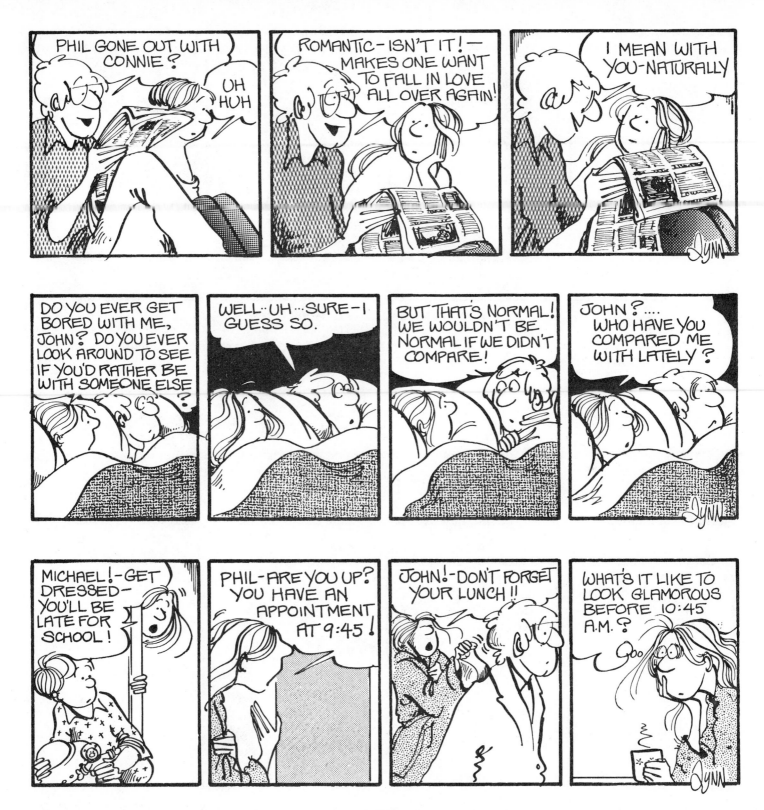

GZZZ-NFFZ Zzz

MADAM! YOUR SON HERE DROPPED A MARBLE INTO MY MOUTH WHILE I WAS SLEEPING!

WHY, MICHAEL?

WELL...UH...

'CAUSE THAT'S ALL WE COULD FIND!

EXCUSE ME— MY BOY WAS HOPING HE COULD SEE THE ENGINEER!

WELL...I—UH... IT WOULD MEAN SO MUCH TO HIM!

BUT, DADDY—I DON'T WANNA SEE THE..MPH!

SHH!

I DO!

WE HAVE AN HOUR BEFORE WE ARRIVE IN VANCOUVER, YOU TWO—SO PICK UP YOUR STUFF.

I DON'T WANNA! NOW! BUT, MA— THAT'S AN ORDER, MICHAEL!

THE ADS ABOUT TRAVELLING BY TRAIN ARE RIGHT, LIZ....

IT'S JUST LIKE HOME.

MICHAEL, HOW LONG HAVE THESE SOCKS BEEN IN YOUR BOOTS?

NOT LONG .... A COUPLE OF MONTHS, MAYBE.

WHAT'S WRONG? —THEY NEED WASHING?

WASHING?!!! — MICHAEL, THESE ARE **KILLER SOCKS!**

I WANT YOU TO CLEAN UP THIS MESSY ROOM, MICHAEL!

UNFAIR! — I ALWAYS HAVE TO CLEAN UP THIS — PICK UP THAT! ...

WHAT AM I — SOME KIND OF **SERVANT?**

I THINK I STOLE ONE OF HER LINES.

OK — I'M FINISHED MY ROOM!

YOU'RE NOT FINISHED — YOU STUFFED YOUR TOYS IN YOUR UNDERWEAR DRAWER — AND YOUR CLOTHES UNDER THE BED.

RIGHT! — THAT'S HOW I'LL KNOW WHERE EVERYTHING IS !!

WHEN SANTA COMING, DADDY?

A LONG TIME FROM NOW, LIZ-ABOUT 13 MORE SLEEPS.

HIM MAKIN' STUFF RIGHT NOW, HUH, DADDY? HE WATCHING ME FROM THE NORF POLE!

I THINK HE'S A LITTLE CLOSER TO YOU THAN THAT!

ELLY, DID YOU TELL MICHAEL ABOUT SANTA?

HE WANTED THE TRUTH, JOHN.

WHAT DO YOU SAY WHEN A CHILD ASKS YOU FOR THE TRUTH?

"LATER".

NO, ELIZABETH, CHRISTMAS IS STILL A LONG WAY AWAY!

IT'S DAYS AN' DAYS AN' DAYS TO WAIT.

I BE ALL GROWED UP BY THEN!!!

WHATSA MATTER, MICHAEL?

MOM AN' DAD ARE SHOUTING AT EACH OTHER.

WHY YOU CRYING? DEY NOT SHOUTING AT YOU!!

I WISH THEY WERE... THEN MAYBE I COULD UNDERSTAND IT!

WHERE ARE YOU GOING? OUT!! SLAM!!

AND I'M NOT COMING BACK TILL I'VE COOLED OFF!!

KNOCK! KNOCK!

I'VE COOLED OFF.

WHAT'S HAPPENING NOW, MICHAEL?

UM.... SHE SAID SHE'S SORRY — AND NOW THEY'RE HUGGING.

WHEW... AM I EVER GLAD THAT'S OVER!

PARENTS ARE GREAT TO HAVE, ELIZABETH. BUT THEY CAN DRIVE YOU NUTS!

WHY IS IT THAT ALL OF YOU HAVE TO PLAY WHERE WE ARE?

CAN'T ANNE AND I HAVE A DECENT, ORDINARY CONVERSATION WITHOUT ALL OF YOU IN HERE?

THAT'S BETTER!

NOW.... WHO WERE WE TALKING ABOUT?

..SO, CONNIE STILL SEES TED, BUT CARES ABOUT PHIL, PHIL'S WRAPPED UP WITH GEORGIA, WHO'S 7 YEARS YOUNGER THAN HE IS....

AND - OH, WHAT IS IT, MICHAEL? CAN WE BREAK FOR A COMMERCIAL ANNOUNCEMENT?

ME AN' CHRISTOPHER AN' 'LIZABETH WOULD LIKE A DRINK.

THANKS..... YOU MAY NOW RESUME NORMAL PROGRAMMING

IT'S MINE! IT'S MINE!

IT'S MINE! MINE! IT'S MINE!

IT'S MINE! SNAP! IT'S...

....IT'S YOURS.

TIC! TICKA TAP!
TIK TAPPITY

---well, that's all the news I can think of, Mom -
I'll leave some space - Elizabeth wishes to
add a few lines.
Love Elly

p ppk g g3 3 3zzzz8! !& 0 0 0S S SMi i i i j j i j j
f f f f f f f f f f f b b b b? ?2 2222 7 7 7 !!& o o o o u u u
L L L d d d c c c caaaaaE E E E E E E F E E E E ...

CAREFUL WITH THE PACKING, ELLY...

LAST TIME I WENT TO A CONVENTION - YOU FORGOT MY RAZOR, MY DEODORANT AND MY GOOD SOCKS.

THEN WHY DON'T YOU PACK YOUR OWN SUITCASE?

...BECAUSE YOU DO IT SO WELL!

SMACK

CAN I COME, DADDY?

NO, MIKE - IT'S JUST A LOT OF MEETINGS... YOU WOULDN'T HAVE ANY FUN.

BESIDES.... WITH ME AWAY - YOU GET TO BE THE "MAN OF THE HOUSE!"

BILLS BILLS

WORK! WORK!

COULDN'T I JUST BE "THE OLDEST KID"??

HAS DADDY GONE?

YES, HONEY.

HE TOOK AN EARLY PLANE - SO WE'LL BE HAVING SUPPER WITHOUT HIM.

IT ISN'T THE SAME WITHOUT DADDY, IS IT? - WE'RE GOING TO MISS HIM AREN'T WE?

UH-HUH.

CAN I HAVE HIS DESSERT?